*When you feel me in your heart
Just look up...
I will be right here...*

they cross over the River of Dreams on the Rainbow Bridge. They believe that on the other side of the bridge, the animals become healthy and young again and play with their friends while they wait to be reunited with their families and friends…
We believe it, too. John, Teri, & Patrick

Contents

"F" is for Forrest 5

Forrest's Foster Family 8

Forrest Finds His Forever Home 10

Forrest Meets Jenny (Just Like Peas and Carrots) 12

Forrest Gets to Know His New Mom 16

Forrest Gets His Wheels 20

Forrest Helps Animals In Need 24

Forrest's 13th Birthday 27

Forrest Crosses the Rainbow Bridge 29

Forrest Meets Grampa and Hanu 33

Forrest's New Friends 36

Forrest Meets Bear 40

Forrest and the Beach 43

Forrest and Hershey Get Ready 46

Forrest Learns to Surf 49

Forrest and the Beach Party 52

What Forrest Learned 57

A Message from the Authors 60

Acknowledgements 61

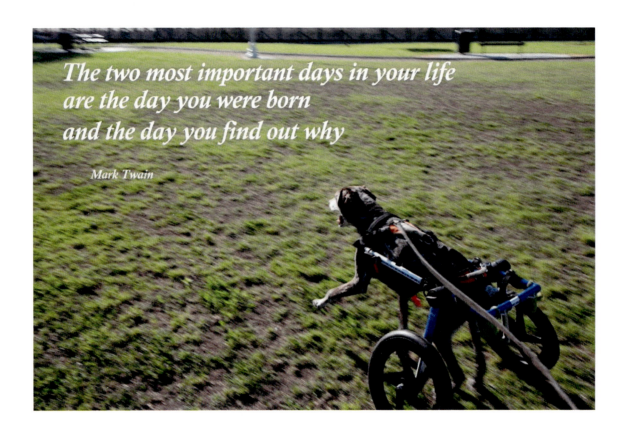

"F" is for Forrest

Everyone is different! That's what makes YOU so special!
Dr. Seuss

My name is Hanu. You will read about me later in the book, but first I want to tell you a story about a dog named Forrest who, despite facing many challenges, never gave up.

Forrest didn't have such an easy beginning in his life, but because dogs live in the moment, he was able to forget his past and find happiness with the help of his friends, a kind-hearted animal rescuer, and a very special family.

Hanu

Forrest's story began alone on the busy streets, until one day a woman saw him. She noticed that he seemed sad and scared, so she approached him very slowly. She was kind and spoke softly to Forrest to be sure not to frighten him. Forrest looked at her and thought, "She has a very friendly face, and she has treats!" He came closer. She began petting him, and he kind of liked it! The woman then noticed a marking on his forehead and began tracing her finger around what looked like the letter "F." Forrest had always been embarrassed by this mark on his head. He thought it made him look silly and not like everyone else. The woman told him how special he was, that the mark on his forehead made him unique, and certainly not like anyone else—and that was a good thing!

She told him she was going to name him "Forrest." Little did Forrest know that not only did he receive a new name that day, but he was about to get a brand-new life.

Forrest's Foster Family

Forrest and Dude

Forrest's rescuer did not have a foster home available for big dogs like him, but a woman who fostered Chihuahuas offered to take him in if they all got along. Thankfully, there were no issues, and Forrest had a place to stay while he waited for his new family to come and adopt him.

Forrest was a bit shy, but he wanted to make friends and be a good friend to others. Sometimes, when he was alone on the streets, other dogs didn't want to be Forrest's friend, and that made him sad. The Chihuahuas didn't know what to think when a big dog like Forrest came to live with them.

One of the Chihuahuas was named Arthur, and he constantly growled and barked at Forrest. One day, Forrest had an idea. He gently put his paw on Arthur and licked his head. The barking and growling stopped for the rest of Forrest's stay there. Arthur later told him that he and the other Chihuahuas kept barking because they were afraid of Forrest. When they found out Forrest wasn't going to hurt them, they all became friends and even played ball together. Forrest had always been the one who was scared—he never imagined that anyone would be afraid of him. Sometimes, he thought, you have to show others that you are nice if you want them to be nice to you.

Forrest Finds His Forever Home

One day, a man named John was looking on his computer at shelter and rescue dogs who needed a home, and he spotted Forrest's picture.

The picture reminded him of the dogs that he'd grown up with, and he remembered how much he and his family had loved them.

His rescuers had named him Forrest. It seemed logical. It was as plain as the "F" on his head. John fell in love with Forrest as soon as they met, and he adopted Forrest that very day. Forrest not only got a new Dad, but he also got a brother and two sisters! The two girls, Baby Girl and Nikki, looked very similar to him, but they were white with brown spots. The boy was named Buster, a dog who was small like Arthur, the

Chihuahua he met when he was rescued. They became a family and played together all the time! Forrest fit in like he had been there all his life. He felt loved and safe, and he was very happy!

As the years went on, Forrest welcomed many other dogs who came to visit. John helped a rescue group when they needed someone to drive dogs from animal shelters to a place where they would be loved and cared for until they found a forever home, just as Forrest had. Sometimes the dogs would visit for a couple of days until they could make the trip to the rescue. Forrest was always kind and friendly to them. He made sure that they were comfortable, sharing his toys and showing them how to use the dog door to get to the backyard to play and go to the bathroom. Forrest knew that everyone wants and deserves to be loved.

Forrest and John

Forrest Meets Jenny (Just Like Peas and Carrots)

Many years later, John's other dogs had gone to the Rainbow Bridge, and he and Forrest missed them terribly. Forrest didn't like to be alone, and John knew that he needed a friend. Forrest and John went to the German Shorthaired Pointer rescue, and they noticed a pretty little dog who looked a lot like Forrest's sisters, Baby Girl and Nikki. Forrest seemed to like her, and she liked Forrest. They played together for a while, and then Forrest looked up at John and gave his paw of approval that she was "the one." She

Jenny and Forrest

was going to be Forrest's Jenny, just like in the movie "Forrest Gump"! When they were at the rescue, they also met Jenny's friend Teri, who was a volunteer at the rescue.

Not only did Forrest find Jenny, but

Forrest and Kelsey

soon after, John and Teri got married, and Forrest got a new brother named Kelsey and a new sister named Hope!

Forrest was tolerant, but also cautious. Very soon, he and Kelsey became best friends. For Kelsey, that was huge—he was very shy and didn't really know how to be friends with other dogs, which was lonely for him sometimes. Forrest made a big difference for Kelsey, teaching him to trust another dog and that life was so much better with a buddy.

Forrest Gets to Know His New Mom

We don't stop playing because we grow old
We grow old because we stop playing
Forrest

Forrest loved to go for walks, just like every dog! Daily exercise is so important to be happy and healthy! It is also a great way to bond with your best friend! Teri would take Forrest on walks just the two of them every day. Forrest was a prancer and a sniffer and was also a little nervous when he heard dogs barking from behind fences. Teri held him close and told Forrest that she loved him and would keep him safe.

Forrest wanted to sniff every flower on their walks. He would look up at Teri with his beautiful golden almond eyes as if to say, "No need to rush, just enjoy the sun and the breeze and all of nature surrounding us." Forrest showed his family that there are beautiful things all around and that we should all take the time to enjoy them.

Forrest loved to have fun! He was full of GSP energy even as a senior. He LOVED to play ball and chew on his other toys. Whenever someone came to his house, Forrest would greet them at the door, say hello with his deep bark, then run to the toy box to grab a

Teri and Forrest

toy. Every. Single. Time!

Forrest, Jenny and Hope

Forrest NEVER stopped moving! There are photos of him that are just a blur. One photo in particular was taken when he was playing fetch with Jenny and Hope. In the photo, Jenny and Hope are standing there, and right behind them is this blur that looks almost like a cartoon character.

Forrest didn't like having his picture taken! He would be sitting there quietly and Teri would come up to take his picture. He would suddenly let out his huge bark and scare Teri, making her jump! When Forrest ate, he sometimes left some food on his nose. Teri would laugh and say, "Hey Forrest, you have a little something on your nose." He would look at her as if to say, "Yes, Mom, I know. I'm saving it for later!"

Forrest LOVED cucumbers, and whenever Teri made a salad, he'd come into the kitchen and stare at her until she gave him a few slices.

Forrest Gets His Wheels

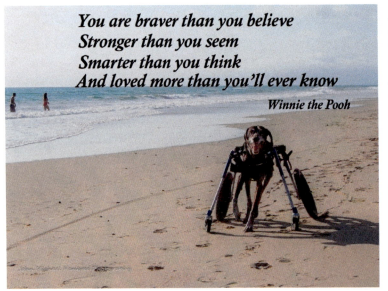

As the years went by, Forrest started having trouble walking on his back legs and he needed help getting up. The doctors told Forrest's Mom and Dad that he had a disease that made it difficult for him to walk. But Forrest never let it bother him. Other than a couple of legs that didn't work so well, Forrest was a very happy boy. Forrest's Mom and Dad heard there were wheelchairs for dogs just like there are for people, and they decided to buy him one to help him walk. At first

Jenny, Hope and Forrest

Forrest didn't want to use it. He was afraid and embarrassed. He thought the other dogs might make fun of him and his wheels. But after walks to the park and along the beach, he realized that his wheels were helping him, and no one who saw him made fun of him—they thought he was very brave, and they loved watching him run and play. From that day on, Forrest was lightning on wheels, and there was no stopping him!

The first time Forrest went to the beach with his wheels, there was a surfing contest taking place. Some people who were watching the

 surfers spotted Forrest and his wheelchair and came up to say hello. They were curious about Forrest and his wheels. They asked why he needed them. They said they had dogs with similar problems who were also having trouble walking. After meeting Forrest, they decided they wanted to get wheels for their dogs too! Forrest looked up and smiled. He thought to himself, "I have nothing to be embarrassed about having a wheelchair. My being in a wheelchair at the beach that day showed people that it's okay to ask for help if they

need it. Especially when it can improve your life. The best part is that I just helped some other dogs!"

As Forrest and his mom and dad continued walking along the beach, some kids approached them and asked what was wrong with him. They said they felt sorry for him. Forrest smiled up at the kids, and they began petting him. Forrest's Mom said, "You shouldn't feel sorry for him. He is a very happy dog." From that day forward, Forrest was happy to go everywhere in his wheelchair.

Forrest Helps Animals In Need

If you see someone without a smile give them one of yours!
— Forrest

One of the reasons I think Forrest is so special, said Hanu, is how he tried to help and inspire others by showing them that, with the help of his wheels, he could still do what other dogs could do.

Forrest was rescued and adopted, given a second chance to be in a loving home. Forrest's mom and dad wanted to help other animals have that chance, and they joined Team California GSP Rescue in an event called "Race for the Rescues."

The event included many activities, along with a one-mile dog walk and kids' fun run.

Forrest walked into the wind and over the rough rocky ground in his wheelchair because he knew he had a purpose: to participate for those that were depending upon him who couldn't. When Forrest crossed the finish line, kids came over, wanting their picture taken with him. Forrest raised the most money for the team!

This event helped save the lives of dogs, cats, horses, and marine mammals too! Forrest's participation raised awareness and inspired pets and people with physical challenges that they can do most anything others can do!

Forrest's 13th Birthday

Forrest began to slow down and was getting pretty tired. We had just celebrated his 13th birthday, which is 91 in people years. You see, dogs don't live as long as people do. Their life on earth is much shorter. Someone once said, "Everyone is born so that they can learn how to live a good life, to love everybody, and be nice to others. Animals already know how to do that, so they don't have to stay as long."

One night, shortly after his 13th birthday, Forrest, surrounded by his family, peacefully went to sleep and crossed the Rainbow Bridge.

Forrest Crosses the Rainbow Bridge

Just when the caterpillar thought the world was over it became a butterfly!

When he woke up, Forrest found himself walking across a beautiful bridge, next to many other animals and people walking together. Forrest introduced himself to a beautiful, fluffy cat walking next to him. The cat said "Hi Forrest, I'm Blossom. It's very nice to meet you."

She and Forrest were both looking at the beauty that surrounded them. The air was fresh and clean and Forrest felt strong and healthy. He looked back and realized that he was walking without wheels! He saw

Blossom

Blossom and the others restored to health and they started running across the bridge together.

Suddenly, dogs, cats, birds, iguanas, and all kinds of animals rushed on to the bridge past Forrest. A happy chorus of squeals mixed with barking, meowing and chirping erupted as the animals greeted their loved ones.

Forrest looked ahead and saw a beautiful meadow where a river met the sea. He leapt onto the soft grass from the bridge, and he ran and ran. As Forrest was running toward the beach, it reminded him of a special place that he remembered on Earth. He stopped when his paws felt the sand between his toes. Closing his eyes, he sniffed the salt air and listened to the sound of the waves and the seagulls and kiwi birds.

"Hello, Forrest." Surprised to hear his name spoken softly next to him, Forrest opened his eyes and saw two dogs smiling at him. "Welcome to the other side of the Rainbow Bridge. My name is Rusa. Klaus and I are here to welcome you. You will meet many other animals and humans here, but the first greeting is always made by someone who will be known to you."

Rusa

"What is this place?" asked Forrest.

"It's where we wait for our family and friends," replied Klaus. Forrest heard some excited barking and turned to see his sisters Baby Girl and Nikki

Klaus

Kelsey

Buster

and his brothers Buster and Kelsey running up to greet him. The reunion resulted in a flurry of wagging tails.

Klaus continued. "Some of us return here many times to greet companions when they cross. Just as our humans may have had many pets throughout their lives, many of us have belonged to more than one family, or have had a special place in the hearts of other people. If we loved them, and we were loved by them in return, we will be here to greet them when they cross." Forrest smiled.

Nikki

Baby Girl

Forrest Meets Grampa and Hanu

"Come follow us," said Klaus. He and Rusa led Forrest and his brothers and sisters toward a tree in the meadow.

All the people and their animal friends gathered around the tree, where there was a man standing on a patch of raised ground. Just as Forrest and his friends arrived, the man began to speak.

"Welcome to the other side of the Rainbow Bridge. My name is Grampa John, but you can just call me Grampa."

Grampa John

A monkey jumped out of the tree, landed next to Grampa, and shouted, "My name is Hanu!" He looked around at the crowd and said "We'll show you wonderful things and teach you some of the secrets of this place." Hanu then began to shake the tree and what looked like leaves began to fly away. Everyone realized the "leaves" had been butterflies. The butterflies hovered over Forrest and all the other new arrivals. They began to flutter and float about dancing in the air. Soon the butterflies were joined in their dance by birds, bees, and dragonflies. Hanu began to play a ukulele and started singing a song. Daisies, daffodils, and sunflowers began to sway along keeping time with the music. The animals all played together during the song. They laughed when they saw that a butterfly had landed on Lucy's nose.

After the song ended, Forrest walked up to Grampa. "I feel that I know you."

"We never met on Earth, but I have been connected to you ever since my son John adopted you." Grampa wrapped his arms around Forrest and hugged him.

Lucy

Forrest's New Friends

Open up your heart to others
The more you love
The bigger your heart will grow

The new arrivals gathered around Hanu and Grampa. Hanu talked about the kindness that all creatures in this place show toward one another. The old disagreements between animals are forgotten.

"Take some time to introduce yourselves," said Hanu. "In a little while, we will tell you more about this place."

A black and white cat tapped Forrest on the paw and said, "Hi, my name is Oreo. My mom and dad called me that because they liked Oreo cookies, and they thought I was as sweet as the cookie."

Hershey

A small German shepherd sat down next to Oreo and said, "My name is Sophie. My parents named me that because it means 'wise,' and they thought I was a smart puppy."

A dog came up to Forrest. "Hi, my name is Hershey."

"Hi, Hershey," replied Forrest. "It's very nice to meet you."

Arthur, the Chihuahua that Forrest met when he was in a foster home, was a new arrival and ran up to the group. "Hi Forrest, remember me?"

"Arthur!" exclaimed Forrest. "Of course I remember you!"

After a short while, Hershey nudged Forrest. "Take a look at Hanu. Is he okay?"

Hanu held his chin with his right hand and scratched his head with his left foot while he balanced himself with his left hand and right foot. He had his eyes half-closed and his mouth slightly open. It looked like he was half-awake while dreaming about something funny that made him grin. The animals were looking at Hanu with puzzled looks on their faces. They started talking quietly among themselves, wondering what had happened, when Hanu opened his eyes.

"Stop chattering and follow my example. I'm going to teach you all how to meditate. All you need to do is breathe in and breathe out. Try not to think about anything, but if you do, don't worry about it. Just let the thought go back to wherever it came from. If you want to think about something, think about this. By making friends with yourself, you make friends with others. By hurting others, you hurt yourself."

Grampa chuckled to himself as he saw all the animals learning how to meditate. Soon they were all sleeping side by side. Grampa sat under the tree and thought how peaceful it all was. Soon he was napping too.

Forrest Meets Bear

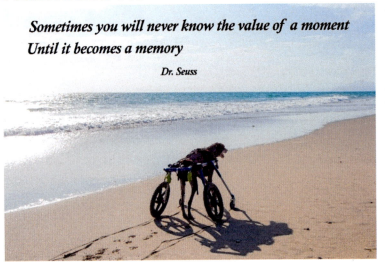

Sometimes you will never know the value of a moment Until it becomes a memory

Dr. Seuss

When Forrest woke up, there was a little Jack Russell Terrier who had joined their group. Forrest's friend, Prince made the introductions. "This is my friend Mick. He belonged to my Dad's sister Colleen."

Mick was very excited. He was going to be reunited with Colleen shortly. A horse pranced up to the group and stood alongside Mick. "My name is Buck. Colleen fell off my back when she was a little girl and broke her arm. I never had a chance to apologize, and she didn't get to finish her ride." Mick spied Colleen in the distance. He couldn't restrain himself, and he ran onto the bridge. He jumped into her arms. She hugged him and kissed him. She smiled when she saw Prince. "I remember you. I'm sure Patrick will be very happy to see you when he crosses over the bridge." She looked at Buck. "Who is this? Wait, it can't be. Are you the horse I fell off of?"

Buck nodded and said, "Guilty." He then knelt down so that Colleen could climb onto his back. They all headed toward the other side of the bridge.

Bear

Forrest watched them for a while and then turned just in time to see a dog walking toward him. They were drawn to each other, but they didn't know why. "I feel that we are connected somehow," said Forrest. "Who are you? I feel a connection too," replied the dog. "My name is Bear, and I was loved by two little girls named Kenzie and Alli."

"I know them," replied Forrest. "My Dad called them 'the Munchkins.' My mom Teri must be very sad, because her daughter and Kenzie and Alli love you very much." They touched noses, and a tear ran down Forrest's cheek.

Forrest and the Beach

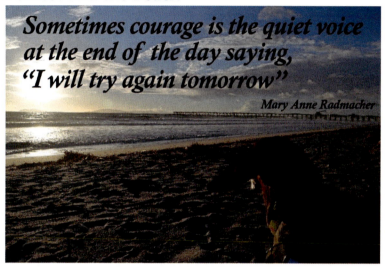

Surf dogs Kanga and Ruby rode a wave in to shore after surfing all morning. They walked up to Forrest, who was lying in the warm sun with Hershey. Ruby shouted to the boys. "Hi guys, do you want to borrow our surfboards and catch a few waves?"

Forrest laughed and looked at Hershey, who looked at the waves, then at Forrest. "Have you ever tried it, Forrest?"

"Not yet," replied Forrest, "but I'm going to try it soon."

Kanga did a quick shake to dry off. "You boys just let us know when you'd like to learn and we'll be happy to teach you."

Hershey smiled. "That sounds like a plan!" The girls ran off to grab some lunch, having worked up a big appetite.

"You know, Hershey, there was a time when I would never have thought about surfing, or even just being near the ocean," said Forrest.

"When my dad first adopted me, he took me to the beach near our home. The waves were so loud that it scared me, and I pulled against my leash to tell him that I wanted to go back to the car."

Hershey tilted his head. "I would never have thought that you were afraid of the waves. You spend so much time here at the beach."

"Well," said Forrest, "my dad kept bringing me back and showed me that the noise wouldn't hurt me. Pretty soon I was even walking on the shore and letting the waves touch my paws."

Hershey smiled, "I'm glad that you're not afraid anymore. I like it here!" "Me too," replied Forrest. "We had a lot of fun at the beach."

Forrest and Hershey Get Ready

Grampa asked all the animals to gather around at the beach so he could tell them they were going to have a beach party. There would be many activities, including surfing lessons for anyone who wanted them. Hershey ran up to Forrest. "Here's your chance, buddy!" Forrest replied, "Cowabunga, dude!"

Hershey tilted his head. "Forrest, are you all right?"

"Totally, dude!" smiled Forrest, "I'm just really amped. It's crankin' and we can catch some epic waves! I just hope we don't look like Barneys out there!"

Hershey tilted his head around the other way, "Forrest, I'm pretty worried about you right now."

"I'm okay, Hershey," replied Forrest. "I've been studying up on how to talk like a surfer."

"Okay," said Hershey, "what did you just say?"

Forrest laughed. "I said that I'm very excited, the waves are really good, and I hope that we don't look like we've never surfed before."

"But Forrest, we HAVEN'T ever surfed before!" replied Hershey.

Forrest winked. "I know that, and you know that, but THEY don't know that."

"Okay, buddy," replied Hershey, "let's find Ruby and Kanga and start practicing."

Kanga

Ruby

Forrest Learns to Surf

For the things we have to learn before we can do them, we learn by doing them!

—Aristotle

Kanga and Ruby were just bringing their boards to the beach when the boys ran up to them.

"Hi, boys," said Ruby. "Are you ready to learn to surf?"

"Yes, we are," answered Forrest excitedly.

"What do we do first?" asked Hershey.

"Let's walk out over to where the water is calm and practice standing on the surfboards," said Kanga.

Forrest followed Kanga out a few feet as Hershey did with Ruby.

"Okay, Forrest. I'll hold the board still, while you climb on," urged Kanga. Forrest carefully climbed onto the board, trying to steady himself as the surfboard wobbled under him. Kanga tried her best to hold the board still, but Forrest slipped off the board into the water.

He shook himself off and laughed. "That's harder than it looks!"

"Hey, look at me!" Forrest looked up to see Hershey standing on the board. Forrest was just about to say something when Hershey shouted, "Uh, oh," lost his footing, and fell into the water.

He came up laughing, determined to keep trying until he could stand up on the board without help.

There was some good-natured laughing coming from the shore. Grampa John and the puppies were watching. "You guys are doing great! To get good at anything takes practice. Just listen to the girls, and you'll be riding waves before the end of the day."

With encouragement from Grampa John and instruction from the girls, Forrest and Hershey were soon getting on the boards and balancing without help. "Okay, boys," said Ruby, "You're doing great. Let's walk down the beach and try riding some ankle busters."

Forrest and Hershey tilted their heads together. Kanga laughed. "Ankle busters are little waves."

The boys kept practicing and listening to the girls' instructions, and pretty soon they were both riding small waves side by side.

Forrest and the Beach Party

*When you wish upon a star
Your dreams will come true*

Jiminy Cricket

The day of the beach party arrived. There were many activities, and everyone was having fun.

Horses and mules raced through the surf, sending water into the air with each step. The splashes they made with their hooves made little rainbows in the drops of water.

Cats were playing badminton, swatting the birdies with their paws. Blossom leapt high into the air to make sure that nothing got by her.

Baby Girl, Nikki and Prince were chasing Frisbees thrown by some of the many people who had come to join the animals for the party.

Hanu was throwing tennis balls for Ochi and a group of dogs on the beach. Blue, the Coon Hound, would catch one and roll all over it. Bengal was showing off that he could hold 3 tennis balls in his mouth! The dogs splashed joyfully in the water to retrieve the balls. They made a game of shaking the water off next to Hanu. Soon the monkey was as wet as the dogs. He pretended to be irritated, but he was having as much fun as they were.

Blue

Bengal

Ochi

Sage

Sage grabbed a towel off of the beach and started a spirited game of keep-away with it

Grampa was watching the dogs taking surfing lessons. Ruby and Kanga, along with many other dogs who had learned to surf on Earth, were busy giving lessons.

Forrest and Hershey, having learned to surf before the party, were trying to surf together on the same board.

Oliver

They fell into the water many times, laughing at themselves as they learned to be a team. Dolphins gave Forrest and Hershey rides on their backs to catch up with their board and try again. Soon they got to where they could ride the waves in to shore without falling. They even invented a new pose where they would both raise one paw and point together on the board. Forrest shouted, "Grampa, this is for you!" Grampa laughed when he saw the boys showing off.

At the end of the day, the animals gathered together to enjoy the sunset. They talked about how much fun they had and what they would like to do at the next beach party.

After the sun went down, Forrest lay down next to Kelsey in the soft grass. He thought about his family on Earth and could feel their love for him as he drifted off to sleep. That night, he dreamed that he was walking on the beach in his wheels; he looked around and saw other dogs in their wheelchairs walking beside him. They felt the sand between their toes and breathed in the scent of the salt air. The warmth of the sun felt good on their backs, and the sounds of the waves and the kiwi birds filled their ears. It was a good day to be a dog. Forrest smiled.

*Even if we are apart,
I will always be with you*

Winnie The Pooh

What Forrest Learned

Forrest faced many challenges in his life. He went from being alone, feeling embarrassed by a birth mark on his forehead, to meeting someone who told him he was unique and special. He learned how to turn a bully into a friend. He

learned to accept his disability and turn it into an ability to inspire others. He faced his fears, and learned that with patience, love and a little help, he could do just about anything.

Most importantly, Forrest learned that no matter how hard it was to walk, no matter how many times he would fall down, he always got back up and landed on all four paws. He never complained. He always had a smile on his face, he was always happy and full of joy, excited for each new day. He was grateful for his family

and friends who were always there to help him. Even when there were days Forrest struggled, giving up was not an option. Forrest taught us that even when we are having a bad day, to get up, dress up and NEVER give up! If there is something that you want to become in life, something you have dreamed of, but you run into obstacles along the way like Forrest did, don't stop trying, and don't give up. Stick with it because you CAN do just about anything you want to do! Always believe in yourself, and NEVER give up on your dreams!

A Message from the Authors

Always be loving to your furry, feathered, and finned friends, and treat other living beings with compassion. By showing kindness towards animals, it will help you be more considerate in your relationships with people.

There are many ways to help animals. Since Forrest was rescued from an animal shelter, we thought this was a good one to start with.

Donate to a local animal shelter or rescue

You can make a difference for animals by collecting and donating food, blankets or making handmade pet toys for shelter dogs and cats. By practicing being a good citizen, you can help change the lives of homeless animals in need.

Acknowledgements

Surfdog photos courtesy of (c)Karen Hight, DogPhotog.net

Surfdog Photos of Kanga, Ruby and Oliver courtesy of Greg Williams – CA GSP Rescue

Made in the USA
Las Vegas, NV
01 October 2022